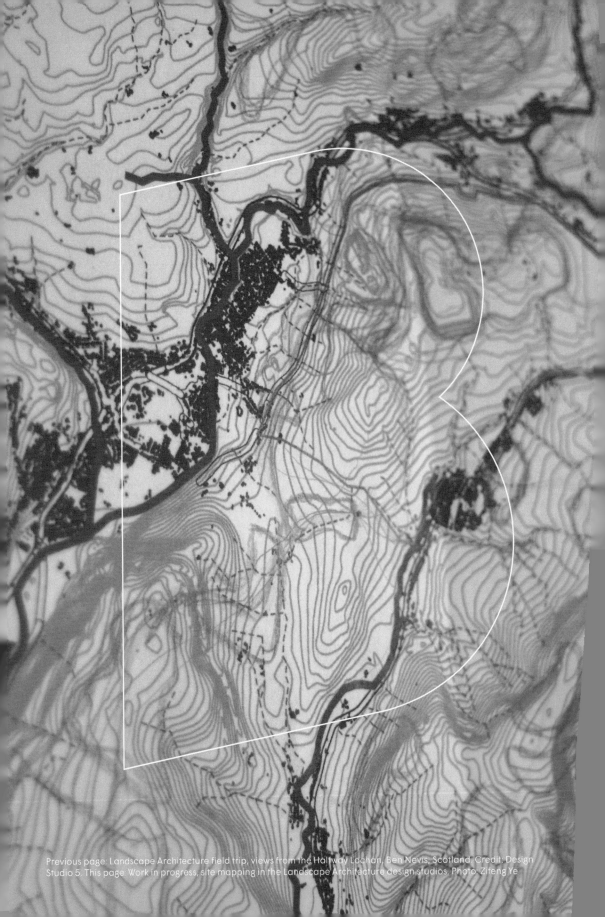

Contents

Introduction

I am both excited and grateful for this opportunity to introduce the provocative work of the students in the Architecture & Historic Urban Environments and Landscape Architecture Master's programmes at The Bartlett School of Architecture. While unique in their pedagogical framing, these programmes share numerous affinities. Both introduce students to complex and creative processes of the documentation and analysis of culturally constructed sites. Both utilise research and design methods that negotiate with existing systems and infrastructures, positing the work of design as engagement in its myriad contexts rather than the mere production of objects. Both position the activities of design and research within a broader expanse of planetary time that is simultaneously ecological, geological and historical. And both leverage a detailed understanding of these deeper historical conditions in anticipation of new design futures that are socially, racially and environmentally just.

The projects in The Bartlett Autumn Show 2022 are a testament to the agility and resilience of our staff and students who produced this innovative work amid a devastating global pandemic. In this sense, the student work is engaged in contemporary matters – material and ethical, historic and futuristic, physical and virtual –

as an expression of what *matters* to them as designers. As Donna Haraway writes in *Staying with the Trouble*, 'It matters what matters we use to think other matters with; it matters what stories we tell to tell other stories with; it matters what knots knot knots, what thoughts think thoughts, what descriptions describe descriptions, what ties tie ties. It matters what stories make worlds, what worlds make stories.'

This year is particularly exciting as, for the first time, The Bartlett Autumn Show is being displayed in a dual format – both online as part of our digital exhibition space and on site at our Bloomsbury home at 22 Gordon Street.

On behalf of the school, I would like to thank all the students, staff, alumni and industry partners who, together with a huge extended network of family and friends across the world, have worked so hard to make the show and this book a reality. To the students who worked so diligently to bring to fruition the projects displayed in this book, thank you for showing us what *matters* to you, *what stories make worlds, and what worlds make stories.*

Amy Kulper
Director of The Bartlett School of Architecture

Nida, Architecture & Historic Urban Environments MA field trip to Lithuania, 2022. Photo: Ana Ximena Garcia Roldan

Architecture & Historic Urban Environments MA

Architecture & Historic Urban Environments MA

Programme Director: Edward Denison

We are living in a time of planetary crisis and transformation. A century of unprecedented population growth, urbanisation and migration has imposed unsustainable pressures on the planet and heralded an entirely new geological epoch: the Anthropocene. Whether working in ancient cities or ultra-modern metropolises, the greatest challenge facing built environment professionals in the future will be adapting and improving what already exists, not building anew.

Rising to the challenge, this multidisciplinary programme promotes a fresh and rigorous approach to the city in the 21st century. Focusing on the themes of environmental, racial and spatial equity, students are encouraged to engage critically and creatively at any scale and through any media to re-evaluate, rethink and restore historic urban environments, making them more resilient, equitable and sustainable.

Working alongside design tutors, historians and researchers with unique global experiences and diverse perspectives, students examine cities from around the world, using London as an outstanding laboratory for learning. The work presented in the Autumn Show is a selection of the final projects which build on the knowledge and experience gained throughout the year in a combination of core and elective modules. These include wide-ranging thematic lectures from guest speakers, site visits to a variety of buildings and landscapes, and specific skills workshops, such as 3D scanning and model making. With the world-renowned Survey of London team, students learn the processes of urban surveying, recording, mapping and analysis, alongside strategies and key issues concerning urban and cultural heritage.

In conjunction with developing a robust theoretical and practical understanding of different sites and analytical methods, students are encouraged to become tomorrow's leaders in the built environment professions, thinking critically and working creatively to cultivate their own mode of practice that seeks to realise a better future built on the past.

Students
Chandrima, Sisi Chen, Daniel Timothy Patrick Davis, Paula De Castro Mendes Gomes, Michael Howard Egan, Ana Ximena Garcia Roldan, Sema Nur Gul Guldemir, Aisha Hassan, Ajmona Hoxha, Wenjie Hu, Carlos Andres Huerta Fernandez, Jude Jabali, Francisca Lopez Pani, Frista Puspita Marchamedya, Claire Elaine Robey, Hanna Nicole Sepúlveda Armuelles, Xiaowan Shen, Jiamei Song, Kıvılcım Göksu Toprak, Karla Alexis Vich, Xi (Amanda) Zhang

Tutors
Eva Branscome, Ben Campkin, Sarah Dowding, Emily Mann, Maxwell Mutanda, Thomas Parker, Lakshmi Priya Rajendran, Jane Wong

Postgraduate Teaching Assistant
Amr Elhusseiny

Supervisors
Peter Bishop, Jonathan Kendall, Guang Yu Ren, Shahed Saleem

Skills Tutor
Danielle Purkiss

Programme Administrator
Drew Pessoa

Image: Ninth Fort, Kaunas, Architecture & Historic Urban Environments MA field trip to Lithuania, 2022. Photo: Carlos Andres Huerta Fernandez

1.1 Paula De Castro Mendes Gomes 'Ocupações: A Viable Way to Introduce Social Housing in the City Centre of Belo Horizonte'. This project looks at the existing vacant buildings in the centre of Belo Horizonte, Brazil, and explores the possibility of repurposing them as social housing as an alternative to the existing housing policy of the country.

1.2 Ana Ximena Garcia Roldan 'From Urban Void to Cultural Production: An Accumulation of Cultures in Centro SCOP'. This project investigates how the heritage of Centro SCOP, an abandoned complex in Mexico City, can be preserved by maintaining and restoring the original site and by projecting its national identity to an international audience through a range of artistic and architectural practices. The project introduces the cultural heritage of indigenous communities to the site in a self-sustaining productive settlement that fosters spatial identity by bringing together cultures in a temporal arrangement, thereby creating awareness about the significance of indigenous culture in Mexico.

1.3 Xi (Amanda) Zhang 'Bringing Back the Bell'. This project is based on research into the gasworks located near The Oval, London, and the surrounding community that is predominantly made up of black and working class inhabitants. The project proposes a design approach that could be used as a case study for other gasworks throughout London.

1.4 Xiaowan Shen 'Recovery from Ghost City'. The project combines the post-pandemic phase of human recovery with the environmental and ecological changes in the city itself. The project transforms the city into a sanctuary where vacant residential buildings are converted into spas for tourists to relax and unwind from stress.

1.5 Jiamei Song 'New Sensory Museum Bridging Death and Memory'. This project re-evaluates modern attitudes to death through a study of Brompton Cemetery, London. By exploring everything from burial activities to spiritual memorialisation, the project looks at how London has evolved and how death has impacted the city. The architectural design uses space to convey how people's reaction to death progressively changes and becomes part of the city's memories.

1.6 Wenjie Hu 'Rebellious Urbanisation'. This project focuses on the Hmong people, an ethnic minority who live in Guizhou province, China. The project investigates the culture shock that they have experienced due to the national rural development policy of poverty alleviation relocation (PAR) and how this policy is negatively impacting their traditional culture and wellbeing. Based on these investigations, an adaptive housing project is proposed, designed to balance the cultural autonomy of the Hmong people with the PAR development policy within the project area.

1.7 Sema Nur Gul Guldemir 'Rethinking Contested Heritage Within Urban Imaginaries/Beirut: The Egg'. Before the civil war in 1975, Beirut was the centre of tolerance for different denominations and cultures in the Middle East. However, the civil war triggered class divisions and sectarian conflicts. This project focuses on the Egg, a concrete modernist ruin abandoned to its fate in the turbulent past of Beirut.

1.8 Hanna Nicole Sepúlveda Armuelles 'Reviving the Old Town of Belchite'. This project examines the importance of reinhabiting abandoned towns after wars and proposes ways to reconcile and honour the identities of survivors for future generations. Through analysis of militarily displaced populations and post-conflict reconstruction, a new design approach is proposed.

1.9 Sisi Chen 'Boundary of Liverpool Chinatown'. The project traces the boundaries and examines the definition of 'ethnic enclaves' – geographic areas with large migrant populations which include a number of business owners from that community. Such areas have multiplied with the advent of globalisation as more and more diverse communities have migrated around the world over recent decades.

1.10 Claire Elaine Robey 'The Grenfell Tower Fire'. The project is an illustrative interpretation of the data supplied in the official written report following the 2017 Grenfell Tower fire in the Notting Dale ward of North Kensington, which resulted in the deaths of 72 people.

1.11 Chandrima 'The Way I See It'. This project is a hybrid research and design proposal that examines the built environment, both existing and proposed, from a woman's perspective. The project studies the similarities and differences in spaces considered the safest or most dangerous to women, the parts of a city where women feel comfortable and the parts women avoid.

1.12 Francisca Lopez Pani 'Fill in the Blank: Creating Spaces for Social Interaction'. Situated in Jardín Ramón López Velarde, Mexico City's second-largest public park, this project explores the concept of the void as the leftover space that results from the chaotic accumulation of urban layers of rapid obsolescence. The park has been neglected for decades as a result of this ongoing phenomenon.

1.13 Karla Alexis Vich 'Reframing Mestizo Identity among the Post-Colonial Remnants of Mérida De Yucatán'. The project focuses on neglected or abandoned buildings in the urban fabric of Mérida, Yucatán's Centro Histórico, which is layered with Maya and Spanish colonial architecture. The area is a designated cultural heritage zone and legislation prevents any visible interventions, modifications or additions to its historical buildings.

1.14 Michael Howard Egan 'All the Things on Wandsworth Road'. This project encourages a more holistic approach towards architectural conservation and building/site listing processes, one that acknowledges the benefits and collective value of the normal, ordinary and everyday features of an urban environment by celebrating the specific character and culture of Wandsworth Road and its residents.

1.15 Aisha Hassan 'Inherited Heritage'. This project explores the scars that industry has left on Luton's built environment and how this has impacted notions of heritage in the town today. The methodological and theoretical approach of the project centres around participation, relying heavily on the involvement of not only others but also oneself. By collecting and analysing an array of oral history interviews, the project focuses on the lived experiences linked to Luton's industrial built history, touching on themes of migration, demolition and memory.

1.16 Kıvılcım Göksu Toprak 'Istanbul's Lost Leisure Spaces as Collective Memory Superstructures: Relearning from Meadows and Beaches to Overcome Social Polarisation'. The project examines how social relations within a community are constructed and how boundaries are negotiated through everyday encounters and appropriation of space. The research focuses on recreational spaces that have the potential to sustain autonomous, spontaneous, self-iterating interactions between individuals in a community. It takes two of Istanbul's lost leisure typologies – 'free' land activated through temporary occupation – as case studies: *mesires* (meadows) and *plajs* (beaches).

1.2

1.3

1.4

1.5

1.6

1.7

1.8

1.9

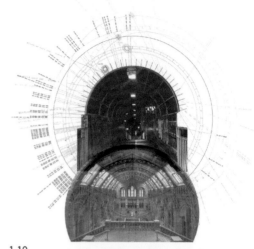

1.10

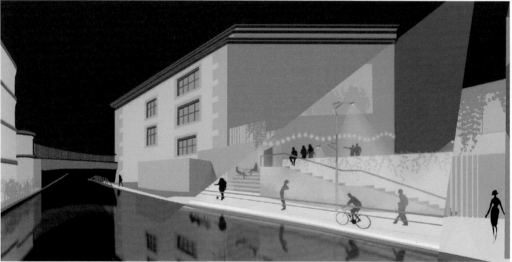

1.11

1.12

1.13

1.14

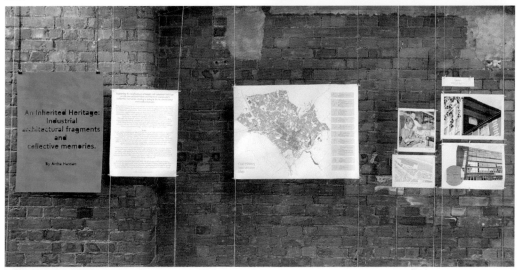

1.15

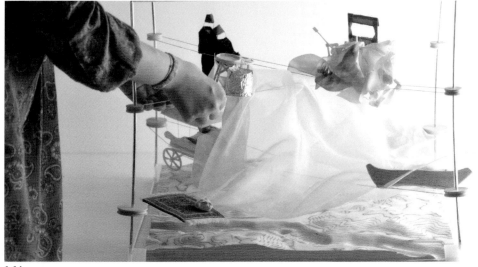

1.16

Indonesia's New National Capital City: Consolidation in the Everyday
Frista Puspita Marchamedya
Supervisor: Peter Bishop

Indonesia is moving its capital city from Jakarta in the island of Java to East Kalimantan in the island of Borneo, purportedly because Jakarta can no longer sustain itself. The proposed masterplan and draft law are contentious and the project is regarded by some as being infused with colonial and Western values, with little to no regard for existing communities. The utopian nature of the megaproject is detached from the reality of the everyday and is, in some ways, already showing signs that history is about to repeat itself.

There are insinuations of colonist gestures towards the existing settlement that bear a resemblance to the approach taken by the Dutch colonial government in Batavia which ultimately led to the doomed position Jakarta faces today. When entrenched in the law, this ideology can manifest in the form of physical urban space that, despite original intentions, might turn into a form of segregation and create urban enclaves.

Due to the inaction of authorities, marginalised residents have also taken it upon themselves to improve their living conditions as a way of remaining in, and belonging to, the city, yet the spatial uncertainties faced by these local people who rely on such spaces for living and working have not been ameliorated.

To bridge the gap between the development of the project and the present reality, this thesis proposes a reappropriation of the draft law to ground its execution in everyday urbanism and its spatial ability to consolidate.

Image: Photo montage of East Kalimantan, Borneo. Image by the author

Whose Estate? The Case for Saving Central Hill
Daniel Timothy Patrick Davis
Supervisor: Shahed Saleem

Since 1997, regeneration has resulted in the full or partial demolition of more than 160 council estates in London, leading to the displacement of over 55,000 households, or approximately 150,000 to 200,000 residents. This is urban transformation at a scale never before seen in London, and as such it is a topic that has already been richly researched. This study exists to complement the scope and breadth of this scholarship, shedding new light on the themes of the arguments made thus far – from gentrification and displacement to power, agency and heritage – by framing them against the experiences of residents, campaigners and neighbours at and involved with a single site of investigation: Central Hill Estate in Lambeth.

The work examines the complexity apparent at the scale of just one London estate, chosen because it is currently at risk of demolition. It describes the complicated and often opaque range of actors and groups that acquire the power to drive decision-making with respect to the future of such estates, questioning the motivations for, and validity of, this power. It also documents the impact of the confusing decision-making process that often follows, and then uses this evidence to explore whether the future of these estates could, going forward, be handled better by those responsible for shaping it.

Ultimately, the purpose of this work is to concentrate the mind on one primary line of enquiry: does the situation at Central Hill suggest that it is acceptable to demolish London's council estates, or should this process be opposed?

Image: Edited drawing from Central Hill's original planning application, Lambeth Council (1966). Perspective from the 'Development Brochure'. Image by the author

Navigating Indigenous Nostalgia: The Struggle Over Iqrit, Palestine
Jude Jabali
Supervisor: Emily Mann

During the 1948 Nakba ('catastrophe' in Arabic), the Israeli army ordered the Palestinian inhabitants of Iqrit to temporarily leave their village. In their absence, the military destroyed the village to prevent residents from returning, leaving only one church intact. Since then, Israeli governments have enforced spatial control policies in the area with the aim of eliminating Palestinian cultural and built environments. As a resistance strategy and to counter these actions, Palestinians continue to invoke the past through popular memory, heritage preservation and oral history. But while invocations of the past have proven to be generative for indigenous struggles across the globe, these invocations can become detrimental when they become entangled with the colonial politics of recognition.

Internally displaced within what has become the country of Israel, third-generation Iqriters offer a novel approach to notions of historiography and the built environment. Having watched their elders fight to return to their home through political and legal apparatuses, all to little effect, in 2012 a group of Iqriters transformed the surviving church into a liveable space and returned to the village to initiate new lives based on working the land and cultural activism. In this way they began to reanimate their history and reignite a modernisation process independent of state impositions.

By resituating Palestine within an often-bypassed paradigm of Zionist settler-colonialism and taking indigeneity as a point of departure, this dissertation asks, how do memory and heritage become entangled in colonial politics of recognition to staticise and stagnate indigenous beings? How do Iqrit's third-generation descendants transcend traditional invocations of history towards the production of urban indigeneity and, consequently, self-determination? This dissertation seeks to contribute to critical discussions about architecture and urbanism as political tools both in the creation of, and resistance against, settler-colonialism.

Image: Iqrit, Palestine. فلسطين ،اقرث. Image by the author

The Macroplaza: Reconceptualising the History and Future of Monterrey's City Square
Carlos Andres Huerta Fernandez
Supervisor: Maxwell Mutanda

This project reconceptualises the past and future of the Macroplaza through a series of three short films that narrate alternative and contrasting visions of the square and culminate in a strategic proposal for the future of this controversial territory. Each film poses one of the following questions:

How can the past and future of the plaza be reconceptualised?

How can the experience of the plaza be narrated through different scales and lenses?

What design proposal strategy would allow the plaza to reconcile with the past?

In order to meet an agenda of progress and modernity, the state government ordered the demolition of 40 hectares of Monterrey's historical city centre, including its city square. Shortly after its construction, the new square proved to be unsuccessful in attracting the private investment that justified its existence. In just four decades, evidence of neglect can be found throughout this concrete megastructure. Neither its current course of action nor its complete redevelopment addresses the issues surrounding the square. Nonetheless, a closer examination of its history and present state reveals that the square plays a vital role in constructing the city's identity and undertakes functions that are closely tied to a longer history of the city centre predating the square.

By challenging the name of the square, each film presents the possibility of narrating this territory differently. Focusing on individual stories, memories and future hopes through the 'micro', as well as social structures and discrete fragments of the square, through the 'multi', allows the plaza's story to account for spatial layers that are often overlooked when viewing the square from the 'macro'.

Throughout this project, contrasting visions of the plaza are presented as a way to reflect on the radical differences in how the square can be understood from various perspectives. Based on such methods, a strategy that deals with the overarching research questions is drawn up and narrated through future visions of the square.

Image: *The Macro* (still image from video). Image by the author

Design Studio 7 hiking Hadrian's Wall Path by Steel Rigg, Northumberland, 2022. Photo: Günther Galligioni

Landscape Architecture
MA/MLA

Landscape Architecture MA/MLA

Programme Directors: Laura Allen, Mark Smout

The professionally accredited Landscape Architecture MA and MLA programmes at The Bartlett School of Architecture equip students with critical interdisciplinary knowledge and design skills to work directly at the interfaces of today's urgent ecological, infrastructural and social challenges. Faced with the climate emergency, these programmes respond to the increasing need to work across built and natural environments. Students develop unique skills in landscape research, technical knowledge, strategic thinking and imaginative design. They produce innovative responses to design briefs that support sustainability and deal with real-world challenges such as biodiversity loss, climate change and ecological crisis.

Shown here are the eight Landscape Architecture design studios, all staffed by landscape practitioners, architects, urban designers and academics with distinct agendas. This year, studios directed their attention to landscapes, environments and issues found within the UK. The questions, methods and sites addressed by each studio were broad, highlighting a range of approaches to today's challenges. Themes included responses to the impacts and politics of nuclear power landscapes; speculative methods of designing with the transitional and dynamic nature of changing landscapes; and investigating and experimenting with the notion of rewilding, to mention just a few. The interests of these studios reflect the breadth and depth of the Landscape Architecture programmes and their spatial and intellectual focus.

The design studio is central to both programmes. The studio provides fundamental and specialised knowledge and a strong identity from which students can develop and launch their own approach to the contemporary study of landscape architecture. Design teaching is delivered side-by-side with history and theory, practice, and environmental and technical teaching. Also presented here are excerpts of work from the Landscape Thesis and Environment & Technology modules.

This was a year of change and growth for our programmes. We were profoundly impressed by how swiftly our students adapted to new working spaces and teaching methods, and by their continued and growing commitment to learning and developing challenging, provocative projects. We look forward to enriching that community and our programmes' identity in our new home in Wicklow Street.

We say farewell and thank you to our MA students and graduating MLA cohort. As we say our goodbyes, we embark on a new year of Landscape Architecture and look forward to building on the lessons, knowledge and design experimentation developed over the last year to embrace a greater scope of design, theoretical, technological, cultural, environmental and ecological enquiry.

Year Coordinator
Aisling O'Carroll

Design Studio Tutors
Nico Alexandroff, Kirsty Badenoch, Richard Beckett, Laurence Blackwell-Thale, Tom Budd, Matthew Butcher, Alberto Campagnoli, Emma Colthurst, Pete Davies, Günther Galligioni, Christina Geros, Elise Misao Hunchuck, Cannon Ivers, Doug John Miller, Tiffany Kaewen Dang, Katya Larina, Alexandru Malaescu, Lyn Poon, Danielle Purkiss, Tim Waterman

History & Theory Coordinators
Tom Keeley, Tim Waterman

Thesis Supervisors
Olivier Bellflamme, Albert Brenchat-Aguilar, Emma Colthurst, Gillian Darley, Paul Dobraszczyk, Kirti Durelle, Jon Goodbun, Eric Guibert, Danielle Hewitt, Will Jennings, Marko Jobst, Tom Keeley, Elin Eyborg Lund, Patrick Lynch, Hamish Muir, Andrew Ó Murchú, Anthony Powis, Zoë Quick, Jonathan Tyrell, Adam Walls, Stamatis Zografos

Environment & Technology Coordinator
Ana Abram

Practice Tutors
Maya Abdul-Latif, Aitor Arconada, Vladimir Guculak, Shruthi Padmanabhan, Claudia Pandasi, Samantha Paul, Will Sandy, Tim Spain

Coordinator of Skills & Workshops
Maj Plemenitas

Programme Administrator
Zoe Lau

Image: 'A Journey Across Catchments' composite master plan, Siyu Tong, Design Studio 4

Experimental Disruptions in the Terrain Vague

Design Studio 2

Cannon Ivers, Alexandru Malaescu

We are in a state of climate and ecological emergency. The way we produce, operate and renew our landscape and built environment requires a complete transformation. In *Reciprocal Landscapes: Stories of Material Movements* (2019), Jane Hutton presented the social, political and ecological complexities of material practice, challenging designers to think of materials not as fixed products but as 'continually changing matter that takes different forms',[1] performing beyond the fixed site boundary.

This year, Design Studio 2 focused on climate emergency, placing material provenance, biodiversity loss, water capture and social inclusion at the centre of each project. Students explored unmaking, deconstruction and material reuse, designing disruptions and experiments in the urban landscapes. As Kate Orff, director of the Urban Design programme at Columbia University, states, 'Moving forward, in light of increasing climate shocks and stressors, designing the social must be paired with new forms of architectural expression like un-making, un-doing, subtracting, reversing, decarbonising, tearing out, ripping up, re-planting, softening and connecting.'[2]

Critiquing the international Downsview Competition, Julia Czerniak, professor of architecture at Syracuse University, asked the simple question, 'How much design is enough?'[3] This line of enquiry raises important concerns across the numerous strands of the landscape architecture discipline. According to Anita Berrezbeitia, chair of the Landscape Architecture programme at Harvard Graduate School of Design, 'Landscapes embody at once culture and nature, art and science, the collective and the personal, the natural and artificial, static and dynamic.'[4]

We endeavoured to answer Czerniak's question using 'Terrain Vague' sites as the platforms for design exploration and experimentation. The term 'Terrain Vague' was presented by Spanish architect and theorist Ignasi de Solà-Morales in an attempt to describe seemingly forgotten sites, fragments and leftover areas most accurately identified as 'urban voids': 'Void implies a space of possibility, of expectation.'[5]

We explored sites in the UK and China to develop design strategies for a site of our choosing that fitted the description of a Terrain Vague site as defined by Karen A. Franck in her essay 'Isn't All Public Space Terrain Vague?'[6]

Students
MLA Year 1
Xuan Wang, Ruby
Isabelle Zielinski
MLA Year 2
Wei Ding, Weicheng
Feng, Huiyu Fu, Yan
Gong, Huicong Han,
Qizhi He, Kumphakarn
Sasiprapakul, Binghui Wu,
Mai Xiong, Yizhan (Eden)
Zhang, Yue Zhang,
Minzheng Zhou
MA Year 1
Wenfang Zheng

Practice Tutor
Shruthi Padmanabhan

1. Jane Hutton (2019), *Reciprocal Landscapes*, London: Routledge
2. https://archleague.org/event/climate_change_design_kate_orff/
3. Julia Czerniak (2002), *Case: Downsview Park Toronto*, Munich: Prestel, p14
4. Czerniak (2002), *Case*, p117
5. Sergio López-Piñeiro (2020), *A Glossary of Urban Voids*, Berlin: Jovis Verlag, p120
6. Karen Frank (2013), 'Isn't All Public Space Terrain Vague?' in P. Barron and M. Mariani, *Terrain Vague*, London: Routledge, pp167–84

2.1 Ruby Isabelle Zielinski 'The Dynamic Duo'. The project is centred around changing the narrative of two abandoned dry docks in Henry VIII's Woolwich Dockyard. If left as they are, they stand as a symbol of conquest, defeat and pain. The ships created within them attacked nations around the world in search of more: more power, more land, more riches. What if, instead, it could be a place where people come together? Instead of searching elsewhere, what if the site could attract people to explore more within? This image shows the development of the concept using a lightbox to overlap ideas with a more inclusive use of space.

2.2–2.3 Yizhan (Eden) Zhang 'Pumping Heterotopia'. Abbey Mills Pumping Station in Newham comprises a series of old and modern sewage pumping stations and associated infrastructure. The succession of the pumping station indicates the fluctuating and marginal condition of the site. It also sparks the question of its future. Inspired by Cedric Price's project 'Fun Palace' (1959–61), the project challenges the studio brief by interpreting uncommon human experiences on the site. Given the fact that abundant sewage water and air circulate in the pipelines above and below ground, the proposal envisions an idea to embrace the heterotopia of the pumping station and transform the site into a playful and educational theme park with an industrial stamp, powered by natural forces.

2.4 Huiyu Fu 'Self-Sustaining Testing Ground in the Flyover'. The project uses green infrastructure to renew the fragments and leftover urban areas of a forgotten site under an overpass in London, disconnected by the express traffic lane. The site is located in Canning Town, East London, near the DLR railway track and under the west Silvertown Way Viaduct. At one kilometre long, it is bordered by three major expressways, creating a fragmented infrastructural landscape – one that is defined by operations rather than human experience. The project proposes to rebuild these fragmented linear leftover areas into eco-friendly, welcoming and innovative spaces with interchangeable uses.

2.5 Wenfang Zheng 'Urban Agriculture: New Opportunities and Challenges Under Climate Change'. Climate change is altering every aspect of human life, with agriculture perhaps the most vulnerable of them all. In the summer of 2022, the UK witnessed both the hottest and driest days on record since 1935. This project seeks to reintroduce agriculture to the cities we live in. It envisages a way to combat future climate change through the harvesting and use of rainwater. Through research into water, soil and plants, a 27-hectare derelict site in East London is transformed into an urban farm. The project also retains and reuses some of the landscape elements of the site, such as derelict car parks and gasholders, working with the surrounding community to explore a bottom-up, self-sustaining model of urban living for the future.

2.6 Weicheng Feng 'Deep Museum'. The site is located in Limmo Peninsula in East London – a wasteland after eastbound tunnel-boring machines carried out Crossrail construction. During the construction, workers found the remains of the largest Victorian shipyard in Britain buried underground. After the excavation work, several underground spaces supported by concrete structures were left on the site. These underground spaces retain relatively intact historical remains. However, a large number of waste materials, including broken fire bricks and steel plates, which were considered by archaeologists to have no value, were transported to a nearby landfill site. The project focuses on using recycled materials to reveal the area's hidden history and create a journey through time.

2.7–2.8 Kumphakarn Sasiprapakul 'Realising the Broken World'. A collection of on-site materials plus site analysis and synthesis form a palimpsest with multiple layers that allows the reader to see the fabric of the East London site prior to its design. This includes plants, pavement, water and soil samples from the Channelsea River and surrounding areas. These come together to inform the Museum of Climate Change, where the experimental garden will exist in response to the effects of the climate emergency. Visitors will experience the heat while viewing the Mediterranean and tropical plants that could survive the warm weather in London.

2.9 Huicong Han 'Co-Existence Space'. Shadwell Basin, a part of the former London dock system that includes a tranquil waterway hidden in the city, attracts both humans and wildlife. The project examines how we can create a symbiotic relationship between these two groups in urban spaces with a landscape design that intertwines ecology, economics and culture. The rearrangement of the road system and green space is the primary design strategy. The site has six key landscape nodes, each designed with a different function. These include a commercial area, observation area, leisure area, human-animal interaction nodes, wildlife habitats and educational bases.

2.10 Mai Xiong 'Counter-Monumental Memorial Landscape'. This project is located at Thamesmead, previously the Royal Arsenal – the heart of the British Army during wartime. The project references the three-act structure in designing narrative, aiming to find a balance between the collective memories of trauma and honour. Central to the ambitions of the project is addressing the heritage of urban spaces that have been modernised and those that have been preserved as museums. Christine Boyer, Professor of Architecture and Urbanism at Princeton University, claims that landscape heritage in the mainstream inevitably pushes the scale into a contemporary form of memory crisis. In this context, the narrative practice of design is used to awaken the ghosts of these dormant ruins as a sign of an inherited war along the River Thames.

2.2

2.3

2.4

2.5

2.6

2.7

2.8

2.9

2.10

3.1

Post-Antibiotic Landscapes

Design Studio 3

Richard Beckett, Alberto Campagnoli, Eric Guibert

Our focus this year in Design Studio 3 has been to explore a probiotic design agenda for novel landscape approaches in the Symbiocene epoch through three distinct projects which operated at different scales. We worked according to the post-antibiotic and probiotic philosophy of using life to manage life and explored degraded landscapes as potential sites for increased biodiversity, engaging with non-human agencies as a design driver. Our design responses demonstrated a refined integration between humans and nature across themes including loss of ecological systems and soil degradation.

These strategies were applied to the environment of the UK, one of the least biodiverse countries in Europe. We analysed modern ways of managing life and saw how landscapes, environments and bodies have been degraded by strategies of eradication, control, rationalisation and simplification. We also examined and structured new living assemblages, encouraging human and non-human co-existence.

Projects one and two focused on urban environments in London, starting with overly ordered landscapes in city parks. Our research explored living art, bio-design and modern modes of bio-politics. We stimulated critical approaches and considered access to nature, the emergence of contemporary pathologies and post-Covid pandemic systems in creating novel landscape designs for the Symbiocene era which would facilitate areas of unplanned nature within the city.

In project three, larger-scale strategies were applied and offered a starting point for approaching complex landscapes suffering biodiversity loss as a result of antibiotic management modes. Wales and the former mining site of Nant Helen were used as case studies to investigate post-industrial rewilding and its economic impact on local socio-economic systems.

We speculated on landscapes having potential for co-creation with other non-human probiotic actors and how these new relationships would be beneficial for all living systems. Different agents and their combined effects on ecosystems were carefully chosen for each project, as we researched regenerative empathy as a design outcome to respond to site reuse and rewilding.

Ecological atlases, existing and proposed mapping, storyboards, graphic novels, phenological drawings, videos, animations and physical/digital modelling were among the array of media used to explore and test design processes.

Students
MLA Year 1
Xiaotong Li, Wanying Peng, Tatiana Vera Espinosa, Ziyi Yu
MLA Year 2
Bohan Cheng, Chuyun Gui, Danyang Huo, Zhiqi Tao, Xiao Wang, Yu Wang, Dengcheng Xie, Ning Yan, Menglei Zhang

Practice Tutor
Aitor Arconada

3.1 Tatiana Vera Espinosa 'Regenerative Dimensions of Soil'. This project explores the ecological, social, economic and political dimensions tied to soil for the restoration of Nant Helen coal mine. Permaculture and leisure blend with wildlife corridors, assisting soil care. A new identity for Wales is proposed to recover damaged territory through ecological succession and social collaboration.

3.2 Menglei Zhang 'Post-Mine Regeneration'. The project proposes a landscape community on an existing abandoned open-cast mine located in the South Wales Valleys. This diagram shows the distribution of different functions following the restoration of the mine. Distinct functional zones for humans and non-humans are identified during the process.

3.3 Xiao Wang 'View from Monkey Hill'. In this project viewing decks are built and connected to the ground by steps in the middle of a pit. Due to the height difference, people can safely observe the monkeys living in the low woodland while keeping their distance.

3.4 Dengcheng Xie 'Wetland Detail Plan'. The overhanging walkway offers a route through the wetland and is designed to reduce the impact on the natural environment of both visitors and any disturbances caused by them.

3.5 Zhiqi Tao 'The Spread of Soil Microorganisms'. This map shows how microorganisms reproduce and spread in the soil in response to surface water runoff.

3.6 Yu Wang 'Growth Following Fire'. A wall formed of ivy surrounds the cemetery, guarding the souls of the departed on behalf of their loved ones. The regular layout matches the geometric form of the Victorian era, evoking the image of a Victorian garden cemetery under the moonlight. The division of light and changing surfaces inform the design installation and vegetation configuration.

3.7 Ziyi Yu 'Crossing Rewilding'. The core idea of this project is the duality of agro-paddock and eco-fabric, based on a fierce debate in *The Guardian* about farmers' rights and the rewilding policy in Wales. To achieve a balance, a two-dimensional model of a resilient landscape is proposed. The proposal includes an agricultural pattern with departmentalised economics crossed with rewilding space.

3.8 Tatiana Vera Espinosa 'Regenerative Dimensions of Soil'. Experimental physical mapping is key to exploring the role of soil as a probiotic agent. The Welsh territory is represented as an entanglement of biological and human processes that impact the proliferation of life. A variety of materials and textures are used to portray the complexity of fungal, bacterial and floral networks that develop alongside human activities.

3.9 Danyang Huo 'Using Life to Manage Life: Welsh Ponies in the Rewilding Process'. To address unemployment caused by the closure of the local mine and to improve biodiversity, the native Welsh pony was chosen as an ecological engineer. The design has three dimensions: the pasture provides employment and generates income for the surrounding community; the horse-riding route through the mine creates a special riding experience for visitors; and the movement of the horses in the free-roaming area improves vegetation.

3.10 Ning Yan 'Wilderness of Human and Nature'. A healthy coniferous woodland consisting of dead wood and fungi, veteran trees, old trees, mature trees, juvenile trees and saplings will be restored by the planting practices of locals over a period of time. Old trees with fungi will be installed in an outreach facility to help humans engage with nature.

3.11 Wanying Peng 'Chromatic Riparian Decontamination'. The project proposes a biological hydrological network to reorganise the connection between water and biology at the site. An acid mine drainage remediation system is used to realign the flow direction of the site to form a continuous water network. As a result of remediation, the species in the surrounding environment will start to spread. There will also be a rewilding corridor for species, which will help restore the soil quality of the riparian zone.

3.12 Xiaotong Li 'The Process of Vegetation Movement'. The dispersal of seeds can be calculated by combining research on the wind's strength and direction and the topography of an area. This drawing shows a range of predictions regarding developments in vegetation growth and reproduction.

3.13 Bohan Cheng 'Waterlow Rewilding'. The project takes the Upper Pond area of Waterlow Park in London as a site to explore landscape experiments that combine human and non-human activities.

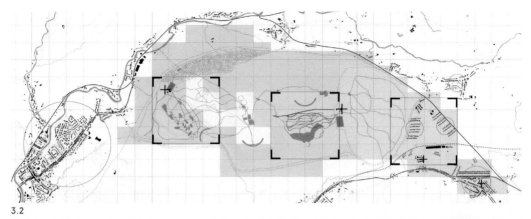

3.2

3.3

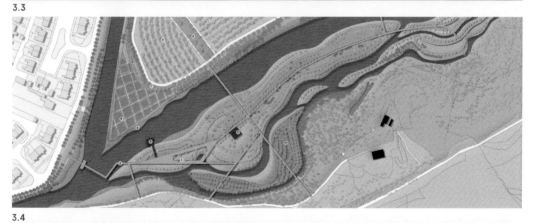

3.4

3.5

3.6

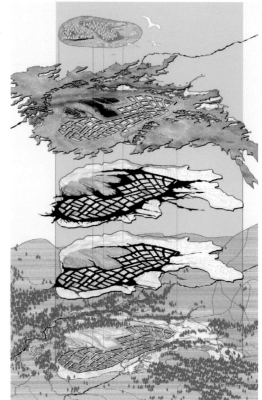

3.7

3.8

3.9

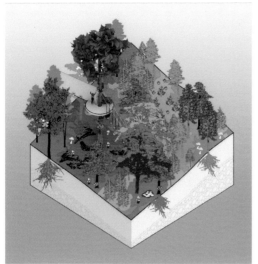

3.10

3.11

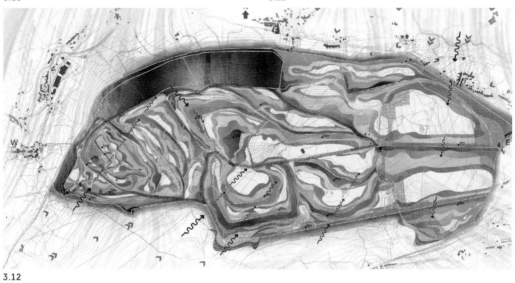

3.12

3.13

Worlds within Worlds

Katya Larina, Doug John Miller

Design Studio 4

Contained and shifted by historical processes, bubbles of ecological wonder spring from the unlikeliest of places. This year Design Studio 4 were inspired by the work of a range of key figures who have influenced the fields of ecology and climate science. Botanical artist Maria Thereza Alves' project 'Seeds of Change', for example, explores the colonial expansion of the 18th century and identifies 'ballast flora' species that bloomed across the world, smuggled in the bows of ships. By contrast, in London a more deliberate transportation of species was developed. Victorian collector Dr Nathaniel Bagshaw Ward invented 'Wardian cases' as a means of transporting miniaturised ecosystems. The ecologies taken and transported from afar in these vessels would be secreted in London gardens or hidden away in private collections.

Now, in the climate emergency, the themes of extraction, display and shielding of landscapes take on new significance. Design Studio 4 speculated on the future of these landscape conditions and how, as designers, we will have to explore new protective regimes and adapt to a rapidly changing biosphere.

This year's brief was inspired by Estonian bio-semiotician Jakob von Uexküll's *umwelt* ('the surrounding world'), and students began by examining the smallest of starting points. In London, a lump of coal revealed themes of historical extraction and unique localised mining legislation. The history of an old pagoda tree was a basis for questions about the evolution of our restoration and collection practices. A slate tile revealed lost memories shared between a London roof and a once-booming Welsh mining town.

Our main projects were located on sites across the world. In each project we sought to address local climatic change, investigate and design with local communities and produce speculative but grounded responses to problems that can only be addressed over long, complex timelines. Each project from this studio represents a student's individual agenda, from the protection of East Anglia's crumbling coastlines to shielding communities and ecologies alike from extreme shifts in water provision in Mexico City. With each project we learned from the complex local *umwelt* to speculate potential landscape futures.

Students
MLA Year 1
Meilin Li, Ian Jing Xin Lim, Elena Tamosiunaite, Bi Ying Wang, Ying Yu (Annette) Wong
MLA Year 2
Ziwen Cao, Chong Guan, Lifeng Lin, Paloma Martínez Solares Callejas, Ziqi Niu, Wanyi Pan, Rasika Patil, Siyu Tong, Yutong Wang, Na Zhang

Practice Tutor
Samantha Paul

4.1 Ying Yu (Annette) Wong 'Rainforest Commons'. Temperate rainforests are lesser-known rainforest habitats that are native to the UK and under serious threat from human activities. Wigford Down is proposed as the pilot site for cultivating rainforest commons. Through strategic regional planning and multiscale landscape designs, a system of landscape infrastructure and a new afforestation technique are developed, transforming commons from bracken-invaded moorland to temperate rainforest with phased management.

4.2 Ziqi Niu 'Parys Mountain: Post-Extractive Ecologies'. Parys Mountain, an abandoned copper mining site in Wales, has a unique post-extraction ecology that can thrive under hostile conditions and process toxins. Using the diverse terrain as a testing ground for mining conditions around the world, the design provides sites for experiments within various environments: steep cliffs, riparian ecologies, mining cavities and sand dunes.

4.3–4.4 Siyu Tong 'Reinventing the Common: The Fen Tigers Roar Again'. A new form of common land is proposed that stems from farm boundaries delineated by constructed ditches once used to drain and privatise the land. This project interrogates the relationships between flood and productivity, authority and autonomy, and aesthetics and wilderness. The proposal suggests the contribution of 'paddocks' tailored to a farmer's needs and seasonal plans. Within the resulting masterplan, local farmers are encouraged to celebrate common customs and traditional construction skills and participate actively to ensure a promising future.

4.5 Na Zhang 'Reciprocal Landscapes'. On the Swanscombe peninsula in Kent, the introduction of a grassland ecology in an abandoned chalk pit becomes a catalyst for wider regeneration. The unique terrain of the chalk cliffs creates a rich habitat across various textured surfaces of the pit. Materials required for the restoration of the chalk pits are extracted from discarded and recyclable materials in the peninsula and help construct a nursery that, from the pit, supplies mature plants to Swanscombe Marshes in the wider area.

4.6 Elena Tamosiunaite 'Freeminers' Bog'. The Forest of Dean was once home to large expanses of valley mire (stretches of boggy ground). This project brings peat bogs back to the forest through interventions to retain water, increase biodiversity, decrease flooding and sequester carbon in the ground. From the Middle Ages to the present day, locals have maintained their right to free mining in small-scale collieries. The proposal transports some of the cultural values embedded in the Freemining culture to the installation and maintenance of the bog. New pathways, wetlands and boggy landscape are introduced by using materials available in the forest, such as natural coal, timber and sandstone.

4.7 Ian Jing Xin Lim 'The 21st-Century Counter-Picturesque'. Situated in the National Trust lands adjacent to Stowe, this project explores the duality of the 'Picturesque' and 'Counter-Picturesque', creating a landscape that provides both picturesque views and a hidden productive landscape. Using technological developments in agriculture, such as pixel farming and automated harvesting, the project proposes alternative pastoral aesthetics of the 'working' landscape.

4.8 Bi Ying Wang 'Plumes and Dunes'. Kessingland Beach in Suffolk is home to a unique dynamic dune system and a coastline under constant threat of erosion. To protect the eroding shingle habitat from further exposure, this project focuses on two approaches to the shoreline. Vernacular sea defence strategies are combined with living dune stabilisation through establishing specialised pampas grass ecologies.

4.9 Wanyi Pan 'Slate Memory'. Grass, meadows and trees are gradually becoming the dominant landscape in Blaenau Ffestiniog, Wales, and traces of the local slate mining landscape are vanishing in the face of inaction. How can the memory of the slate mines be prolonged through subtle intervention as the world and climate change? This project proposes an open form of monument, reviving memories as traces in the living landscape.

4.10 Yutong Wang 'The Mappowder Hedgerow Laboratory'. Hedgerows have been an essential part of British farmland for many years; they mark boundaries, have a substantial environmental impact on the landscape and create linear biodiversity corridors. In a proposed hedgerow laboratory in Mappowder, Dorset, new hedgerow typologies are invented that play key roles in restoring protective boundaries against floods, regenerating original woodlands and grasslands and preserving the cultural legacy of hedgerow craft.

4.11 Chong Guan 'Stoke-on-Trent Ceramic Park'. Stoke-on-Trent's history of ceramic production has left a series of brownfield sites scattered throughout the city. This project proposes the slow and careful regeneration of one site linked to a local park. Through composting organic waste and engagement with local recycling programmes, phases of soil remediation are established and the previously abandoned site becomes a hub of community engagement and ecological sanctuary.

4.12 Lifeng Lin 'The Beddington Beds'. As the energy crisis strikes globally, this project proposes a new landscape form – an experimental energy production park. Located in Croydon, the densest residential borough in London, the park provides renewable energy through large-scale bioenergy recovery while simultaneously promoting an ecological corridor within the Wandle Valley. A combination of wastewater treatment and algae farming is proposed to amplify energy production while treated water is used for wetlands and local households.

4.13 Ziwen Cao 'Daylighting the New River'. As the New River was the first aqueduct in London, parts of it are tucked away in underground pipes, hidden between homes and under tarmac. This project focuses on the participation of the local community in the process of daylighting the river, seeking to restore cultural connections to water, create a sense of place and develop a growing relationship between urban rivers and people.

4.14 Paloma Martínez Solares Callejas 'An Amphibious Utopia'. Cyclical flooding and water shortages affect Mexico City annually. This project proposes a vast intervention within Laguna Mayor's regulating tank. By transforming 22 hectares of earth into seasonal wetland, serious flooding is alleviated through a combination of contemporary and traditional water management techniques. Sustainable drainage systems allow rainwater harvesting, while 'chinampas' grow crops in the outer ponds and retain water in the dryer months.

4.15 Meilin Li 'Industrial Transformations'. Located along the Manchester Ship Canal, this project explores two sites of environmental protection in the face of rising tides. Local salt marshes adjacent to the canal are transformed into an active green flood defence system, while in the nearby Stanlow industrial zone new wetlands are proposed to recover highly polluted territory.

4.16 Rasika Patil 'Healing and Stitching'. The Goyt Valley's peatlands are under threat. Diseased woodlands, hikers and continual extraction of peat have all contributed to the erosion of the valley over many years. A new biodiverse forest, the establishment of a moss garden and the stabilisation of soil structure are proposed to rebuild the valley's ecological diversity and guide hikers away from eroded paths.

4.2

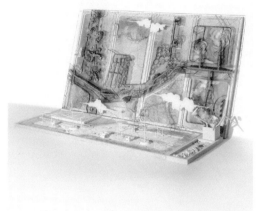

4.3

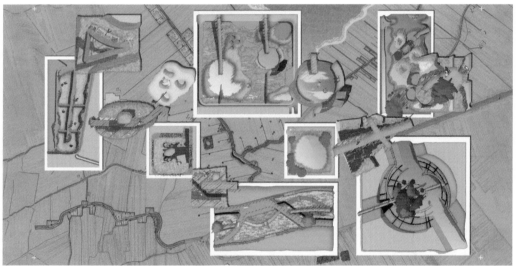

4.4

4.5

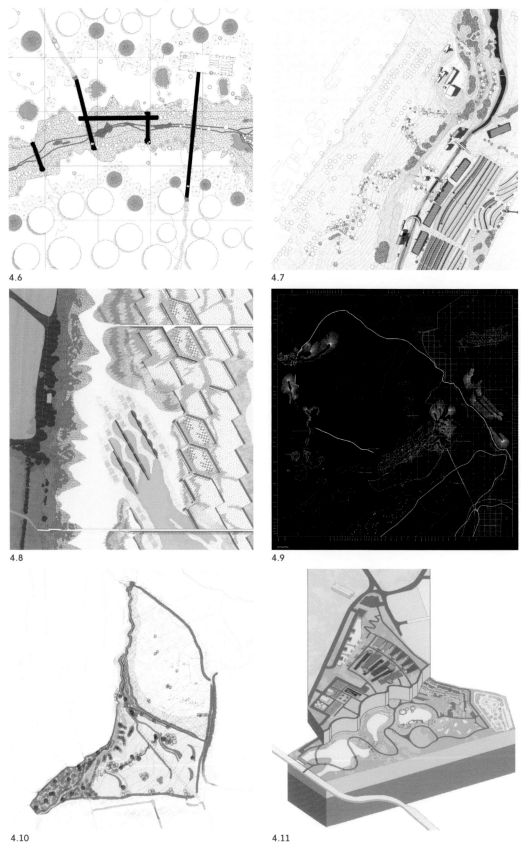

4.6

4.7

4.8

4.9

4.10

4.11

4.12

4.13

4.14

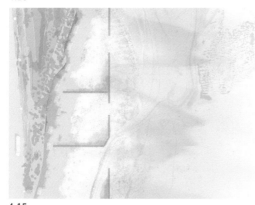

4.15

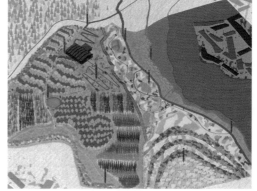

4.16

False Summits

Laurence Blackwell-Thale, Pete Davies

This year, Design Studio 5 have become aeronauts of altitude, questioning what benefits height gives us and at what cost. We speculated on the role of elevation in influencing ecological, geological and technological processes, and how such processes have contributed to 21st-century landscape biomes.

In an increasingly digital world, the ways in which we experience the environment are ever-changing. Digital platforms have enabled us to travel virtually to the highest mountains or to the depths of supposed wilderness with the click of a button. We are therefore interested in how a combination of analogue and digital technologies can augment the ways in which we physically and physiologically explore, experience and understand different environments.

As the starting point for our research, we asked why science, combined with the misty realms of both real and imagined peaks, captivates our minds. While the pioneering ascents of men and women continue to propagate knowledge and progress our understanding and supposed control over the natural world, such investigations are fundamentally futile and error-riddled: looking down from any summit and seeing the landscape from above can bring inaccuracy and will often be scarred by tragedy.

We challenged theories, research and concepts through a process of drawing and making. Curiosity, iteration and testing were encouraged as students developed exciting and rigorous design projects.

The studio explored tools that translate, scale or alter the landscape. These tools could be physical or theoretical, allowing new ways of understanding perception and interaction with the landscape. Many were tested in the field and developed to respond to site-specific requirements.

Our field trip to Fort William, Ben Nevis and the Scottish Highlands allowed us to experience elevation and a range of climatic conditions. Students tested proposals and developed a clear understanding of the challenges elevation creates for landscape architecture. Themes were then expanded into full landscape proposals, allowing students to explore independent research agendas over a range of sites and scales.

Students
MLA Year 1
Xinyue Gao, Yuelin Liu, Ziyao (Jo) Wang
MLA Year 2
Yixiao Duan, Linlin Jiang, Zhounan Lu, Junda Ma, Zhouxin Tu, Dingming Xiang, Yaozhou Zhang, Xiangyi Zhu
MA Year 1
Sutida Wongthiemchai

Practice Tutor
Tim Spain

5.1 **Yuelin Liu** 'For the Sake of Peat: A Landscape for Learning and Conserving'. Historically, within the Scottish Highlands, the cyclical use of peat bred a culture that was closely linked to the land. Through a series of landscape interventions in the peatlands of Cairngorms National Park, the project seeks to promote public access and education about the peatlands and their preservation and restoration, strengthening cultural and emotional attachment to the area.

5.2 **Ziyao (Jo) Wang** 'The Orkney Climate Theatre'. The Orkney Isles, Scotland, are threatened by severe climate risks. This project proposes a performative experience for visitors built on the interaction between landscape, climate and humans. The project depicts landscape tragedies in a theatrical manner, while guided journeys through the landscape present three scenes in the dimensions of both space and time: erosion, collapse and rebirth.

5.3 **Yixiao Duan** 'The Creation of a New SSSI: Transforming Edinburgh's Urban Landscape'. This project re-examines the relationship between urban and natural environments. The site is located in Edinburgh between two sites of special scientific interest (SSSIs), Carlton Hill and Arthur's Seat. The goal is to transform the site into a new SSSI through studies of the ecological environment and innovative design which allow the city to grow and transform sustainably.

5.4 **Dingming Xiang** 'The Highland Heather Burning Landscape Forum'. Set within the rich landscape of the Scottish Highlands, the project proposes a forum to discuss environmental management policies for relevant policymakers, ecologists and travellers from across the world. Drawing on the tradition of heather burning, the project establishes a series of heather landscape swatches which burn at different times of the year depending on the prevailing wind and climate conditions. These swatches demonstrate the environmental impact and benefits of heather burning throughout the seasons for visitors to see, experience and learn from.

5.5 **Xinyue Gao** 'Arran: Travelogue of Scotland – A New Cultural Reserve'. This project focuses on the local legends of the Isle of Arran and strengthens cultural connections by engaging the residents in landscape construction. Rammed earth integrates the rich local material of the area and, through its construction, collapse and reconstruction, create new cultural legends.

5.6 **Linlin Jiang** 'The Lowland Highland Park: A Multi-Generational Landscape Park'. This project recreates the physical and emotional experience of ascending a summit in the Scottish Highlands within a lowland setting, through a series of landscape interventions. Landscape has a strong relationship with human experience and memory. Conversely, similar experiences can help evoke memories of the past. This offers a new way of thinking about the practice of landscape architecture.

5.7 **Xiangyi Zhu** 'Fish Out of Water: Primrose Hill'. This project begins with a study of a fish's eyeball, analysing what the world looks like from a different perspective. The fish's point of view is simulated through a series of ice ball viewing devices situated within the landscape and recorded through 3D-scanned drawings. The drawings are then used to capture the cultural, geological and environmental features of the site that are at risk from the climate crisis.

5.8 **Sutida Wongthiemchai** 'Datum Benchmark Educational Park'. The park is a landscape which attempts to change society's perception of rising sea levels, reframing this from a deadly disaster to a meaningful phenomenon which can be experienced and understood on a human scale. The shifting of sea-level datums provides an opportunity for people, flora and fauna to change and respond and is highlighted and experienced through a series of landscape indicators set across the landscape.

5.9 **Zhounan Lu** 'Centre of Alternative Forestry'. The centre reactivates the commercial forests of Glen Nevis, drawing on the rich tradition of forestry and logging in the area. Different sections of the site become experimental venues for innovation, education and construction, trialling various methods of forestry management. The project creates a space for learning, education and discovery in the Scottish regional forests.

5.10 **Yaozhou Zhang** 'Cradle to Grave to Life: A New-Life Memorial Landscape for Waste'. As construction waste increases in Scotland, the relationship between human beings and waste urgently needs to be reframed. Located in Edinburgh, this project explores how construction waste from the surrounding area can be repurposed for the community. Waste material is processed and reworked into a new landscape, creating parks, woodlands and allotments for residents to enjoy.

5.11 **Zhouxin Tu** 'Loch Lomond Indigenous Regeneration'. Sited on the island of Inchtavannach, one of the larger islands in Loch Lomond, the project establishes a plantation predominantly made up of native oak trees. Reusing dead and dying trees provides good survival conditions for oak seedlings that, over several years, will gradually replace the non-native vegetation on the island.

5.12 **Junda Ma** 'Meteorology Transpiler: An Extension of Sublime Aesthetics'. As landscape architects, can we translate natural and uncontrollable elements into a landscape language that can awaken the sublime spirit? This project is based in Arthur's Seat, Edinburgh, and attempts to simulate the common but elusive meteorological elements that are all around us.

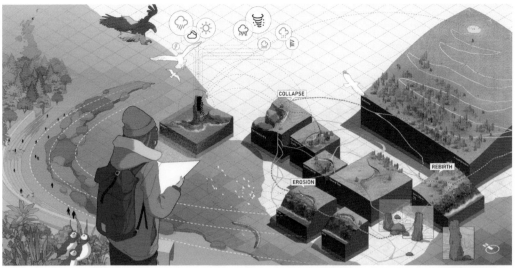

5.2

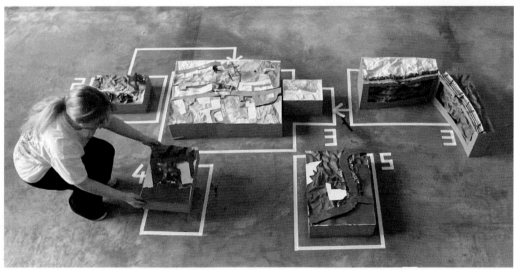

5.3

5.4

5.5

5.6

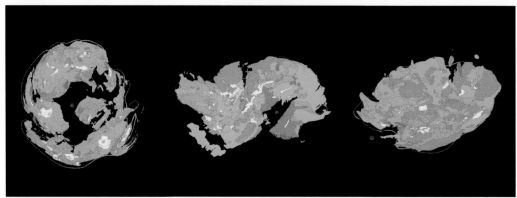

5.7

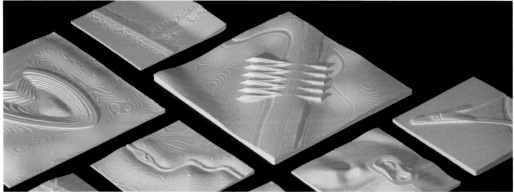

5.8

5.9

5.10

5.11

5.12

6.1

Towards and Against a New Landscape of the Nuclear

Design Studio 6

Matthew Butcher, Tiffany Kaewen Dang

In August 2021, the Intergovernmental Panel on Climate Change (IPCC) released a special report giving an ominous warning about the state of the climate crisis. The report makes clear that there is no longer time to waste in implementing large-scale and systemic changes to slow the planet's rate of warming by reducing dependency on fossil fuels:

Pathways limiting global warming to 1.5°C with no or limited overshoot [will] require rapid and far-reaching transitions in energy, land, urban and infrastructure ... and industrial systems. These systems transitions are unprecedented in terms of scale, but not necessarily in terms of speed, and imply deep emissions reductions in all sectors, a wide portfolio of mitigation options and a significant upscaling of investments.[1]

Alongside the transition to renewable energy sources such as wind, solar and hydro, diversifying energy production into the nuclear industry would quickly and significantly decrease anthropogenic carbon emissions. Therefore, nuclear power can be seen as a transitional strategy to meet zero-carbon energy needs in the short and medium term. Proponents of expanding nuclear energy – at least as a bridge technology to renewables – include climate scientists such as Tom Wigley (University of Adelaide) and James Hansen (Columbia University) and politicians such as American Congresswoman Alexandria Ocasio-Cortez.

This year Design Studio 6 examined how landscape architecture can engage with the infrastructural and political impacts that nuclear power generation has had, and continues to have, on the landscapes in which we all live. Students were asked to consider the past, present and future of nuclear power development – particularly in the context of the UK, where nuclear is responsible for 20% of energy production.

The site of this year's investigation was the Sizewell nuclear power plant and its surroundings on England's East Suffolk coast. The Sizewell plant is formed of three reactors: Sizewell A, a decommissioned plant which was in use between 1967 and 2006; Sizewell B, an operating plant which opened in 1995 and is projected to close in 2055; and Sizewell C, a recently approved and soon-to-be-built project which has attracted much controversy, especially from the nearby RSPB Minsmere Nature Reserve.

Students
MLA Year 1
Ke Ma, Camilla Romano, Yeonjae Yang, Zhuoer Yu
MLA Year 2
Zhuoying Chen, Pin Chu Chen, Dafni Filippa, Haomiao Jiang, Francesca Dawn Lawes, Chuan Liu, Yue Qian, Jinming Wei

Practice Tutor
Claudia Pandasi

1. IPCC Report, August 2021

6.1 Pin Chu Chen 'Decoy/Debate/Deconstruct'. The proposed expansion of the Sizewell nuclear power station in Suffolk has caused much controversy and debate. Inspired by the Þingvellir parliamentary landscape in Iceland, this project proposes to design a number of social and ecological infrastructures to facilitate discourse and discussion on the future of nuclear power. The design of these ceremonial meeting spaces may point towards the democratisation of the decision-making process and test the existing conventions of what forms a parliament can take.

6.2 Yeonjae Yang 'Old Existence, New Connections'. Starting in the Victorian era, an expanded railway network once serviced popular coastal resorts in Suffolk. Today, many of the lines have closed and several beach towns are only accessible by car. This project proposes reopening the Saxmundham–Leiston–Aldeburgh line, with an added tram extension from Leiston to Sizewell beach, revitalising the region's identity as a holiday hub. The new tram line also serves as an ecological corridor, connecting the agricultural fields with the beach dunes.

6.3 Chuan Liu 'The Forgotten'. The present-day Sizewell nuclear power station and nearby medieval Leiston Abbey present a contrasting historical landscape. This project connects these two disparate landscapes by revealing different time dimensions, triggering memories and narrating across space and time. A planting strategy featuring forgotten local botanical plants and a wildlife-driven seed dispersal system links the two sites and creates an ecological connection to the past. The landscape becomes an evocative memory-scape: a historical un-layering of forgotten stories grounded by a botanical revival of the land.

6.4 Dafni Filippa 'Archives of Nuclear Memory and Place'. Following the gradual phasing out of nuclear power, this project builds an archive demarcating the memories of past ecologies under the lens of climate change. The decommissioning processes of the power stations are woven with cycles of growth and decomposition in a ceremonial manner which memorialises the bygone nuclear era of Suffolk. The gradual saline inundation of the site instigates the emergence of buried ecological time capsules, facilitating its transformation into a salt-tolerant ecosystem.

6.5 Francesca Dawn Lawes 'Seeds of Change'. This project is a provocation for the future of nuclear power stations. Facilitated by strategic seeding, the landscape of Sizewell is healed both environmentally and socially, repairing the fractured relationships that have arisen from the controversies of nuclear power. The design creates new ecological habitats and reintroduces life to the coast. The landscape is a stage spotlighting the environmental crisis. The seeds are 'activists', acting as a voice for the landscape and signalling the urgent need for change.

6.6 Camilla Romano 'Landscapes of Scale and Performance'. The vast coastal landscape of Sizewell nuclear power station features incomprehensible scales – the massive structures of the power station have been designed in such a way as to diminish the perceived visual scale of the buildings and blend them into the horizon. This project further plays with perception and scale by using performance and film, engaging the body as a relational tool to explore environmental fluctuations of wind, tide, sediment and time.

6.7 Jiarui Wang 'Follow the Mist'. In place of a new nuclear power station, this project spotlights renewable energy in the form of a bioenergy park. Mist is utilised by various installations to visualise the carbon-neutral energy of the wind, sun and organic matter. The design of the park treats the landscape as a machine to educate and promote the development of renewable energy.

6.8 Zhuoying Chen 'Nuclear Botanical Garden'. As more and more nuclear power plants in the UK are decommissioned, the question of how nuclear post-industrial sites can be sustainably readapted is a significant one. This project proposes a phased transformation of the former nuclear power plants at Sizewell into a botanical garden, using the heated water from the power station's cooling system to raise temperatures in its planting areas. The planting reflects different moments in the history of the nuclear industry and the garden design serves to memorialise the site's nuclear facilities.

6.9 Zhuoer Yu 'The End of the Atomic Age'. Sizewell C will likely be the last nuclear plant built in the UK, signalling the end of the atomic age. This project is a poetic review of this time, reflecting the collective attitudes of fear and hope around nuclear technology. By considering the intergenerational timescales of nuclear energy represented by the 200-year lifespan of Sizewell nuclear power station, this project designs a series of spaces which call attention to the effects of the climate crisis and memorialise the legacies of nuclear power as the atomic age comes to an end.

6.10 Haomiao Jiang 'Invisible Boundaries, Contradictory Aesthetics'. The landscape of Sizewell nuclear power station features an aesthetic of contradiction; there are strong contrasts between the industrial buildings, surrounding nature, coastal erosion, competition between local industries and controversies regarding nuclear energy. This design establishes facilities that make legible the boundaries between the power station and the natural environment from different perspectives, softening the division between humans and nature while restoring the adjacent ecologies.

6.11 Ke Ma 'Urban Salt Marsh Backyard'. The expansion of the Sizewell nuclear power station will damage nearby coastal ecosystems and disrupt the adjacent RSPB Minsmere Nature Reserve. This project proposes to relocate the nature reserve to higher ground, creating a cascade of salt marshes that buffer inland freshwater ecologies from saline intrusion. The design of the marshes utilises tidal sedimentation processes to create a sponge topography that mitigates flood water and reduces erosion. With the new salt marsh, the local economy of the Sizewell region takes on new potential as a saline agricultural landscape.

6.12 Jinming Wei 'Protecting Sizewell through Sedimentation'. More than 40% of nuclear power plants are located adjacent to the sea. To mitigate flooding and erosion risks caused by climate change, this project protects Sizewell power station with natural sedimentation processes along the Suffolk coastline. The project includes a sediment supply system which reinforces a preexisting sub-tidal dune serving as a natural breakwater. The controlled sedimentation patterns also form new islands. Set over a large timescale, this project takes landscape design as a variation process and offers different experiences for people and animals.

6.13 Yue Qian 'From the Tidal Marsh'. In the near future, the freshwater marshes directly west of the Sizewell power station face flooding risks from sea-level rises. This design converts the dying freshwater marshes into a network of salt marshes, combining agricultural and public use. Mussels and saline vegetables are farmed and visitors have the opportunity to experience salt in a variety of ways. The site features a restaurant, kelp gardens and mussel-drying huts. In this time-sensitive tidal landscape, cycles of growing, tasting, wasting and processing determine seasonal occupational patterns and modes of access to each of the installations.

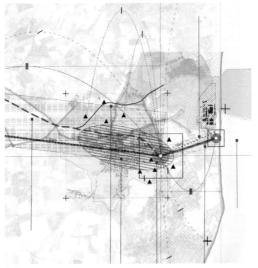

6.2

6.3

6.4

6.5

6.6

6.7

6.8

6.9

6.10

6.11

6.12

6.13

7.1

In Transit, Landscape of Us, as We Move

Günther Galligioni, Christina Leigh Geros

Design Studio 7

At present, only 1% of the Earth is considered uninhabitable because it is too hot. By 2070, however, the overheated, unlivable portion of the Earth is expected to rise to 19%, forcing billions of people to seek new lands to call home. According to a July 2020 headline in *The New York Times*, this climate-predicated migration had already begun, and by the spring of 2021, news outlets were claiming that the previous year had seen more people displaced by extreme climate change than by conflict.

Conflict, migration and weather have a long, entangled history of coercing change across lands. As Eyal Weizman and Fazal Sheikh illustrate in *The Conflict Shoreline* (2015), when weather patterns change, so too does the capacity of the land to sustain the most essential elements of life: the ability to grow food, the availability of water and the various cultural and familial relations that tie us physically and emotionally to the grounds we call home. This year, Design Studio 7 asks how we can design with traces of these essential elements of home and reweave them into the social and ecological fabrics of new identities.

Throughout history, conquered landscapes have carried the marks of their colonisers – transplanted flora and fauna, materials, methods of construction and of marking property, time, health, gathering and dialogue. Largely, the movement of materials and methods can be understood in the context of survival: plants and animals offered known food sources and medicines, framed social relations and comforted homesick populations.

Examples of material exchange between one culture, time or climate and another are so bountiful that they often go unseen. Yet, many of these reconstitutions of landscape have had generations – if not centuries – to settle and be rehomed, so how can we reconcile new recognitions of home while still anticipating change, still on the move and still settling?

With more frequent flooding and droughts, higher land temperatures, fewer clouds and intense and unpredictable storm patterns, the rate and scale of human movement will increase exponentially across the globe. How will we design for comfort within change while we are changing?

Students
MLA Year 1
Weijie Bai, Saebom Kim, Xinyue Mi, Tianyu Yu
MLA Year 2
Yilun Cao, Huiyu Chen, Irene Carolina D'Sola Alvarado, Xinwei He, Zhe Ji, Yanli Ma, Yu Tian, Georgia Tranter, Ying Ching (Conny) Yuen, Yue Zhang

Practice Tutor
Vladimir Guculak

7.1 Yanli Ma 'Peony Migration Journey: Ambience, Sensation on Culture and Weather'. For thousands of years, the peony has permeated every aspect of life in China. However, climate patterns show that in the future the peony may need to migrate. Nur-Sultan, Kazakhstan, has one of the most suitable climates for the plant. This project proposes strategies to reinvigorate the design of public realms in Nur-Sultan by increasing biodiversity, wind and thermal comfort, thereby proposing a rich programmatic palimpsest.

7.2 Huiyu Chen 'Save Coconut Island'. Tuvalu, a Polynesian archipelago, has become a symbol of climate change, as its very existence is threatened by rising sea levels. This project challenges current practices of land reclamation to propose more sustainable, empowering and financially viable strategies, involving the use of natural methods, locally sourced materials and native plants.

7.3 Irene Carolina D'Sola Alvarado 'Caracas in Transit: A Path to a Greener Petare'. Caracas sits in a valley of marvellous natural soundscapes which merge with the buzzing noises of the capital. In a densely built urban environment and challenging topographical context, the project investigates strategies to create safe, accessible and programmed public realm interventions along the Guaire River and within areas of informal settlements, reusing existing assets and implementing a design language that stems from vernacular art and architecture.

7.4 Georgia Tranter 'Reconnecting Communities Across the Greenway'. London's multicultural population is set to grow significantly in the future due to climate-prompted migration. This project proposes the Jubilee Greenway as a continuous green spine crossing several East London districts with a rich demographic mix and milieu. This densely forested linear park becomes an opportunity to bring together communities of different backgrounds and levels of affluence while rooting the proposal in a growing capillary network of local green spaces.

7.5 Saebom Kim 'Beyond the Route: Jubilee Greenway'. This project seizes the opportunity to rejuvenate the Jubilee Greenway route by creating a surprising hiking experience through East London. Following in the footsteps of one of England's first female geographers, Isabella Lucy Bird, the project combines the habitats explored in her return journey from Korea with the UK's hardy native species, while offering opportunities for insights into the history of the Greenway sewer construction and providing informal, playful and relaxing spaces.

7.6 Xinyue Mi 'The Migrating Garden'. This project echoes the UK's history of plant collection and migration, which we can still appreciate to this day in botanical gardens such as those in Cornwall. The project stresses the importance of considering the shifting of biomes and habitats due to climate change. Beckton Gasworks industrial site is regenerated as a test site for cutting-edge remediation techniques and as a landing, collection and sale point for migrating plants while providing new uses for residents and users.

7.7 Yu Tian 'The New Edges: Habitat Renewal in Mariculture Ponds'. Qingdao, China, is well known for its production of clams, which plays an important role in ecology, economy and folklore on a regional scale. However, climate change is already impacting the clams' habitat. This project embraces this change by creating climate-resilient landscape strategies in the vestiges of underused fishing ponds, allowing the sea to progressively repossess this man-made waterfront while promoting biodiversity and providing a richer environment for both clams and humans.

7.8 Weijie Bai 'Double-Faced Park: Migrant Tidal Park in East London Brownfield'. The Bromley-by-Bow Gasworks industrial site along the River Lee offers the opportunity to develop a tidal, flood-resilient landscape inspired by the principles of biomimicry and the lotus flower. The existing gasholders are envisaged as pavilions for the discovery of native and non-native marginal landscapes and plants.

7.9 Ying Ching (Conny) Yuen 'Cattle Chronicles'. Hong Kong has become an urban jungle following the rapid economic growth of the 20th century. As the local agricultural industry declined, cow and buffalo herds were abandoned as a result of urban development. From pioneers to wanderers, the fate of these animals changed dramatically as the city developed. Investigating the issue of feral cattle and the existing planning and land policies of Hong Kong, this project reinvigorates the cattle-scape by redefining territories in the disappearing landscape.

7.10 Zhe Ji 'Rehome Tea, Rehome with Tea'. Jinjunmei is a type of tea cultivated in one specific region of China. Temperature rise, the increase of extreme weather events and a shift in humidity levels due to climate change are endangering the tea's habitat and the survival of those who have farmed it for centuries. The analysis of historical climate data indicates a potential new home for the tea and its farmers in Jeju Island, South Korea. The selected site's complex topography is designed to suit biodiverse farming of tea and other crops, while creating an experiential landscape where visitors can educate themselves about tea cultivation and consumption across China, Korea and the UK.

7.11 Yue Zhang 'The Vanishing Farm'. Climate change has been found to have a significant impact on food security. At the same time, microplastics are now widespread in natural ecosystems and regarded as a great concern by scientists (Xu et al., 2020). Using Beddington Farm, Croydon, as an experimental site, the project develops planting strategies to absorb microplastics while reducing the environmental impact of artificial materials on the substrates.

7.12 Xinwei He 'Tangerine Riparian Agriculture and River Flood Control'. This project investigates ways to enhance current agricultural practices in China's riverine landscapes to increase biodiversity and resilience to floods and erosion, as well as ways to empower local farming communities. The tangerine is used as a symbol of a cultural shift towards biodiverse farming methods and to promote change and prosperity in rural territories.

7.13 Tianyu Yu 'The Railway Home'. King's Cross, an industrial site with a dense infrastructure in central London, offers the opportunity to propose a rich programme celebrating the history of the railway as one of the most sustainable means of travel while also mitigating noise and building a resilient landscape strategy.

7.14 Yilun Cao 'Flying and Floating Dreams'. The humble dandelion is often regarded as an invasive species, but the benefits of this incredibly resilient plant are underestimated. This project uses the abandoned fireworks factory and industrial complex in Dartford as a test site for rehabilitating the overlooked genus of *Taraxacum* as a way to restore habitats and remediate low-nutrient, eroded or chemically polluted substrates.

7.2

7.3

7.4

7.5

7.6

7.7

7.8

7.9

7.10

7.11

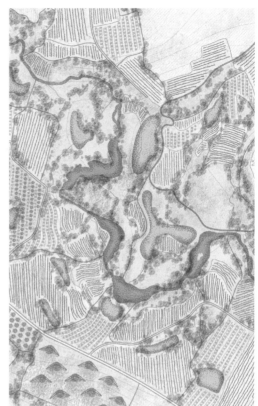

7.12

7.13

7.14

8.1

No Clocks in the Forest

Design Studio 8

Kirsty Badenoch, Tom Budd, Lyn Poon,
Danielle Purkiss

Forests contain untold stories and unread secrets, histories and predictions communicated through complex networks in the soil and through the air. Forests are entangled and enchanted, messy, complex, full of mystery and mythology. They are simultaneously composing and decomposing and are constantly on the move. Forests are misleading, forbidding and wild. If you don't keep your wits about you and your pockets full of breadcrumbs, they could lead you astray and you may never find your way home again.

This year, Design Studio 8 stepped into the woods, cultivating unique understandings of, and relationships with, the notion of time within the forest. Through initial investigations situated within the peri-urban woodlands scattered across London, we sought to frame the forest no longer as an element 'external' to the city, but as the archetype through which to understand it. These investigations looked beyond the physical properties of the sites, exploring the communities, hidden policies and histories that dictated and formed these landscapes. We also examined how the seemingly endless time of the woods sits in contrast to the limited time we have in the face of a looming climate emergency.

Throughout the year, students worked with Flimwell Park in East Sussex. Over a series of visits and workshops across the seasons, Flimwell acted as the studio's *experimentarium* and escape. As a collective we became active agents within the landscape – trailblazing, mapping, foraging and constructing small-scale interventions sited in the surrounding woodlands. These 1:1-scale experiments directly informed the individual design projects carried out in the studio and acted as opportunities for exploration, risk and discovery.

Design Studio 8 look to develop practices of experience-based experimentation, designing through being and doing. We approach the land and city with open minds, embracing accidents and flexing to accommodate unexpected results. We encourage experimentation and challenge standard practice to support an environment of discovery and innovative process and thinking. Fostering a shared and supportive practice, we operate as individuals in a broader ecosystem with a collective purpose.

Students
MLA Year 1
Yingqi (Jessie) Gao, Ana Patricia Garrido Chavez, Blair Ella Kern, Nyima Yangdzom Murry, Chui (Jade) Shan Tsang
MLA Year 2
Qianyuan Chen, Ying Fu, Farinoosh Hadian Jazy, Jinhua Hou, Pinyi Liu, Yu Liu, Jingwen Ma, Xueying Ren, Xinyu Yang, Yue Yin

Practice Tutor
Will Sandy

8.1 Ying Fu 'Rebirth from Decay'. This project integrates decay into design through human intervention on a patch of industrial wasteland in Silvertown, East London. The decay process of the site is accelerated through different strategies to form habitats suitable for various wildlife and human activities.

8.2 Jinhua Hou 'Movable Landscape: Designing for Pandemic Agoraphobia'. As we near the third year of the Covid-19 pandemic, for some, coronavirus anxiety has increased to the point where they are unable to leave their homes. Mental health professionals refer to this as 'pandemic agoraphobia'. This project helps people with this condition by reintroducing them to the outside world through progressive exposure to natural elements, exploring the feasibility of combining and applying multiple landscape elements to heal mental health.

8.3 Ana Patricia Garrido Chavez 'Living Lab Centre'. Situated in the Paddock Community Park, London, this project proposes a living laboratory to test natural methods of soil remediation. The centre is designed to create awareness about how using and discarding construction materials modifies natural ecosystems and how these challenges can become design opportunities.

8.4 Farinoosh Hadian Jazy 'Train-Wind Landscape'. In many cities, green spaces are increasingly becoming fragmented by the construction of infrastructure. To preserve the remaining vegetation in urban areas we need to regenerate the connections between different green spaces. This project proposes creating wind passages in cities through the landscaping and reformation of derelict portions of land adjacent to railway tracks. Trains create artificial wind flows which can improve the wind connection between different green spaces, encouraging the growth and spread of these areas within our cities.

8.5 Group Work 'Filmwell: Collaborative Mapping Drawing'. Throughout the last year, Design Studio 8 has been working with Flimwell Park and the Woodland Enterprise Centre in East Sussex. The area became the studio's *experimentarium* and has presented the studio with an opportunity to physically engage and directly shape the future human and non-human uses, habitats and functioning of the woodland. This mapping drawing represents an initial collaborative exploration within these woodlands, identifying and mapping areas of spatial intrigue and wonder.

8.6–8.7 Group Work 'Flimwell: Trailblazing'. During the year, the studio undertook a series of live workshops and experiments at Flimwell. The first of these looked to reconnect lost sites and habitats within the woodlands through the method of trailblazing. Design Studio 8 became an active agent in the landscape, mapping out these new connections in the first person and working its way upwards from the forest floor. This route marked the beginning of the studio's first steps into the wild.

8.8–8.9 Nyima Yangdzom Murry 'Commoning Epping Forest'. This project seeks to establish a strategy for commoning the formerly public, now private, areas of land around Epping Forest to create a publicly owned landscape that prioritises community management and rights to the forest. This new commoning approach to landscape design was explored and represented through films, drawing, modelmaking and 1:1 workshops.

8.10 Xinyu Yang 'Woodland Walks: A Remedial Landscape'. This project explores the healing power of nature within woodlands and applies these ephemeral qualities to the city. Through a combination of plant species, the project proposes five functional area models to provide different sensory stimuli that establish and strengthen natural connections and have a soothing psychological effect, creating a forest-like refuge in the city.

8.11 Pinyi Liu 'Weaving Friendship'. The number of people seeking asylum in the UK from Europe, West Asia and Africa has risen sharply since 2021. Forced to fulfil its responsibilities towards asylum seekers, the UK government currently only provides extremely scarce supplies and overcrowded spaces in areas far from cities. This project proposes a series of developable islands on the River Thames in the heart of London to provide temporary accommodation and employment for asylum seekers waiting to enter the UK and integrate into communities.

8.12 Blair Ella Kern 'Opportunistic Disruption: The Colne Valley Viaduct'. For hundreds of years, railway development spread throughout the UK, changing the landscape dramatically. Today, it is no different. As construction of the UK's High Speed 2 (HS2) railway commences, impacted communities stand in disagreement. On the edge of London, the two neighbouring towns of Denham and Harefield watch as the Colne Valley Viaduct cuts across ancient woodlands, lakes and recreation sites. This project argues that despite the social and environmental disruption caused by the construction of HS2, the influence of the infrastructure will introduce an influx of funding, ultimately offering an opportunity to re-envision the area, reconnect the neighbouring towns and restore the environment. The project uses chaos as a tool to strengthen a rich ecology and long-standing community, bringing people and other living organisms together in a shared landscape.

8.2

8.3

8.4

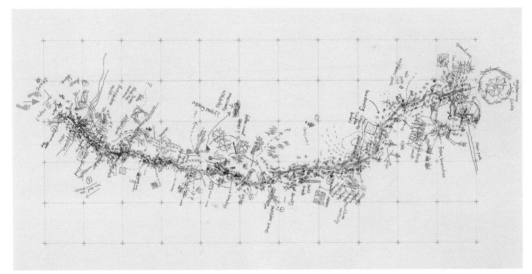

8.5

8.6

8.7

8.8

8.9

8.10

8.11

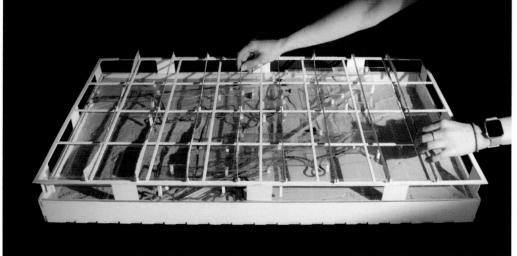

8.12

Forests that Walk: Cartographies of Refusal

Design Studio 9

Nico Alexandroff, Emma Colthurst, Elise Misao Hunchuck, Tim Waterman

Tree planting and reforestation have long been considered the key to tackling the multiple crises of climate change and biodiversity loss. And yet, despite the admirable efforts of initiatives like the Clyde Climate Forest, we see forests everywhere under threat almost entirely due to anthropocentric causes. Forests are migrating – slowly, too slowly – due to changing growing zones caused by climate change.

The forests of North America, Europe, Australia and Siberia are all burning at scales beyond those historically recorded as we move into the age of megafires. In many places, the long history of deforestation by fire and by logging for agricultural practices continues unchecked. The impacts of these events are often far-reaching and extend well beyond the sites of the forests themselves. Yet in some cases, planting the wrong trees – or, paradoxically, planting trees at all – can be worse for the planet's climate.

This year, Design Studio 9 learned not only how to design with forests but how to think with them. To do so, we based our work on the belief, as Jennifer Gabrys argues,[1] that trees are all too often cast as singular fixes for 'wicked problems' – complex, large-scale, planetary problems that are difficult if not impossible to solve. So, how can we respond to wicked problems? Together we returned to the forest, continuing our transdisciplinary investigation into the relationships between research, design and advocacy.

Individually and collectively, we explored multiple forests in the UK and Europe – including Mount Ymittos in Athens, Cefn Mably in Wales and Kielder Forest, the New Forest and Epping Forest in England. Through these explorations, we developed research practices using tools of measurement, representation and communication. We captured the complexity of the multi-layered systems and relations on site, exploring what the role of landscape architecture could be in understanding, mapping and communicating wicked problems. Through design methods, strategies and multi-scalar interventions, we asked: how do we want to live with the forest, and how might we get there?

Students
MLA Year 1
Hera Yuen Tung Chung, Shoshan Dagan, Xinyu Su

MLA Year 2
Tanya Agarwal, Sirapat Ajkarn, Tongqi Cui, Fanzhangyang Jin, Alexandra Souvatzi, Yumeng Sun, Patteera Teeraratkul, Pooja Sanjay Wagh, Dongqi Xu, Bingrui Zhou

Practice Tutor
Maya Abdul-Latif

1. Jennifer Gabrys, 'Smart Forests and Data Practices: From the Internet of Trees to Planetary Governance', *Big Data & Society*, 7(1) (2020): 4. doi.org/10.1177/2053951720904871

9.1 Alexandra Souvatzi 'Oikos of the Pyrocene'. This project envisions a renewed future for Mount Ymittos on the outskirts of contemporary Athens. Currently, its vegetation threatens the expanding suburbs with destruction from wildfires, but this design creates a key metropolitan landscape that hosts social practices and promotes the ideals of pyrodiversity. The wildfires that rule the habitat are tamed, protecting the city through social performance on the threshold between urban and natural environments, in this case along the space of the site's main firebreak road. Social groups from surrounding municipalities are given stewardship of the land to enhance the local economy and to construct innovative methods of forest maintenance, preparing the land for a balanced co-existence between humans and non-humans in the era of the Pyrocene.

9.2 Fanzhangyang Jin 'Reimagining London Communities: Urban Forestry in Pimlico'. A design for an urban forest redefines the neighbourhood of Pimlico through collaboration among its residents. Pimlico is a low-rise, high-density historical neighbourhood. It is perceived to be wealthy but is actually made up of a healthily diverse community. This project uses the historical notion of the forest as a participatory environment and brings it into the contemporary family home. Seven special sites were chosen in Pimlico. Each exhibits building techniques like living walls, scaffolding and street planting to help build a green network across the entire region. The residents join to build a more sustainable environment and create a healthier and friendlier neighbourhood atmosphere.

9.3 Hera Yuen Tung Chung 'Peatland Restoration in Kielder Forest'. This plan provides an overview of the proposed site layout and programme for a river valley in the Kielder Forest, Northumberland. The project adopts a process-based design to restore a historically recognised peatland landscape while addressing its immediate and long-term issues, such as water management, wildlife conservation, tourism and climate change. The interventions cultivate a dynamic forested landscape that experiments with the interrelations between its human and more-than-human actors to preserve the forest's ecosystem against future concerns.

9.4 Patteera Teeraratkul 'Forest for Fungi: Fungi Regeneration through Hydrological Processes'. This project designs a landscape that provides appropriate conditions for the growth of fungi without disturbance from human activity while restoring the ecosystem in terms of the food chain. Access to specific areas for foraging is encouraged and reinforced through design cues and education, while other areas are made inaccessible to serve as a 'bank' for spores and fungi. The design project designs with and for a range of possibilities for life, resulting in the ecological restoration of the fungi population in Epping Forest.

9.5 Dongqi Xu 'Bluebells Blooming in the Sky: Highgate Wood Green Link Design'. In the UK, bluebells are often used as an indicator species to identify ancient woodland. They are also a protected species under threat because of climate change. Protecting bluebells is conducive to maintaining the balance of the ecosystem. Reforestation and protection of bluebells could help mitigate the ecological problems caused by climate change. This project focuses on exploring a natural and effective method for protecting this beautiful bluebell landscape. The construction of ecological links and new habitats enhances the pathways for the bluebells' wind pollination. People are also actively encouraged to grow bluebells in the protection area. The project will help to recreate the blue carpet landscape.

9.6 Pooja Sanjay Wagh 'Curious Woods'. This project proposes the rejuvenation of Parkhurst Forest on the Isle of Wight by establishing a Forest School. The school increases community access to the forest while also encouraging the Forestry Commission to improve management techniques to reverse the area's declining health. The project emphasises the various forms of ecology in a forest and includes creative techniques for teaching children about this ecology. Learning is supported by the design of various zones that focus on water ecosystems, woodland habitats, biodiversity and unstructured play. The school provides a dynamic long-term outdoor learning landscape for other nearby schools, which in turn engages curious young minds.

9.7 Tanya Agarwal 'Hiraeth – A Nature Trail'. The neglected ancient woodland of Cefn Mably is located between Caerphilly and Cardiff in Wales. This project focuses on a nature trail that provides a unique experience for locals and visitors and immerses them in a natural, cultural and educational environment. The local community has an emotional attachment to the area known as *hiraeth*, for which the project is named. This Welsh word describes a yearning for home and homeland and a nostalgia for how things were once. The trail will help people focus on the trees and the intricate ecology of the forest, redirecting this longing into a productive relationship. It will also help visitors realise that the value of the ancient woods is not only ecological but also social, spiritual, archaeological and economic.

9.8 Tongqi Cui 'Coping with Floods: Island-Like Wetlands in the Forest'. The design objective of this project in Queen's Wood, London, is to enhance the forest's resilience to flooding during extreme precipitation in the wet season by creating wetlands along an existing stream channel. In the dry season, these wetlands retain moisture to ensure the growth of surrounding vegetation. The design approach is carried out in three stages. Firstly, wetland islands are created where the stream is blocked by fallen trees, Secondly, an inventory of existing vulnerable trees on both sides of the river is carried out to anticipate when they may fall in a flood and decide what to do with them depending on their size and location. Lastly, 'leaky' dams are made from tree branches and placed in ideal water storage areas.

9.9 Sirapat Ajkarn 'Cwmcarn Forest Renewal'. Cwmcarn Forest in Wales, a recreational destination for families and hikers as well as a source for the timber industry in the UK, has been blighted by the larch disease caused by the microorganism *Phytophthora ramorum*, which damaged and killed more than 150,000 trees in 2013 alone. This project focuses on a massive forest renewal. The interventions include prevention of the forest-wide spread of the pathogen by introducing water canals to extract infected runoff water from the site. Moreover, the planting areas are divided into sectors to support selective logging and further control the disease. Lastly, the pathways are redesigned to balance and reduce conflicts between the key site users: scientists, loggers and recreational visitors.

9.2

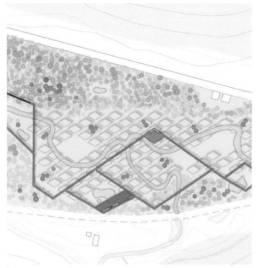

9.3

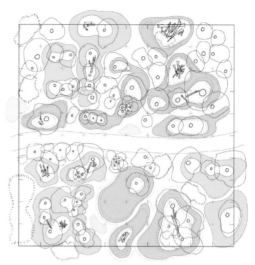

9.4

9.5

9.6

9.7

9.8

9.9

Environment & Technology

Coordinator: Ana Abram

Environment and Landscape Technology teaching at The Bartlett School of Architecture equips students with knowledge, tools and techniques to be able to analyse, preserve, design and construct landscapes of the future. Through two lecture series, delivered by a network of practitioners and specialist consultants who teach a broad range of subjects, and modules, students are introduced to the professional world of being a landscape architect. Subjects such as natural systems, earth sciences, planting design, ecology, climate change adaptation, planning, urban design and construction technologies, amongst many others, are taught and reviewed throughout the year concurrently with design-based modules. Year One students receive an overview and learn about the fundamentals of the subject. Year Two and Master's students cover topics such as climate change, environmental design, landscape planning, conservation and advanced principles in landscape construction.

Landscape, Inhabitation and Environmental Systems
This module sets out the discipline of landscape architecture in relation to physical and natural processes and anthropogenic impacts, and environmental systems – geology, climate and hydrology – are examined. Landscape architecture detailing and the fundamentals of landscape construction are addressed, relating to hard material selection and soil science with planting design. Across three lecture sequences students developed an understanding of why environmental systems matter in contemporary landscape architecture, what those systems mean for built environments and, finally, how to assess and realise landscape projects using contemporary building technologies.

Landscape, Ecology and Urban Environments
This module focuses on topics of climate change adaptation, environmental sustainability, resources crises, environmental assessment and new technologies in landscape architecture. There is a particular focus on the different models of design processes that span from idea to construction. Lectures are supported by extensive seminars, site visits and cross-crits. Modules are enriched by the extensive support of practice tutors, who bring professionalism and a critical view on the buildability of design ideas.

Lecturers
Paola Blasi (ARUP), Elettra Bordonaro (Light Follows Behaviour), Gustavo Brunelli (Atelier Ten), Michael Cowdy (McGregor Coxall), Neil Davidson (J&L Gibbons), Chris Fannin (inSite, HOK), Gary Grant (Green Infrastructure Consultancy), Fred Labbe (Expedition Engineering), Dilip Lakhani (BBUK Studio and LI London), Jennifer Mui (MRG Studio), Donncha O'Shea (Gustafson Porter+ Bowman), Martijn Snob (VOGT), Alexandra Steed (Alexandra Steed URBAN), Steven Velegrinis (AECOM), Harry Watkins (The Bartlett School of Architecture, UCL)

Practice Tutors
Design Studio 2
Shruthi Padmanabhan (Foster + Partners)
Design Studio 3
Aitor Arconada (LDA Design)
Design Studio 4
Samantha Paul (ARUP)
Design Studio 5
Tim Spain (Turkington Martin)
Design Studio 6
Claudia Pandasi (Uncommon Land)
Design Studio 7
Vladimir Guculak (Bradley-Hole Schoenaich Landscape)
Design Studio 8
Will Sandy (McGregor Coxall)
Design Studio 9
Maya Abdul-Latif (AECOM)

Image: Draping Landscapes: Archiving Nuclear Memory and Place. Choreographing growth, decay and decomposition of landscape systems. Dafni Filippa, Design Studio 6

/ Current species are having trouble adjusting to increased saline atmospheric and geospheric conditions.

Detail 1

(Power Station Decommissioning Phase: Removal of spent fu

/ Chitosan-pectin membrane in solid state.

(Power Station Decommissioning Phase: Radioactive Dec

/ Chitosan-pectin membrane while decaying.

(Power Station Decommissioning Phase: Fil

/ Chitosan-pectin membrane final decomposition of remaining flax fibers.

phasing plantation

/ Species 1 / Species 2 / Species 3 / Species 4 / Species 5 / Species 6 / Species

system decay

History & Theory

Coordinators: Tom Keeley, Tim Waterman

The history and theory strand of The Bartlett School of Architecture's Landscape Architecture programme provides a robust foundation, tying together the ideas behind the built landscape and the resulting forms across time, from the scale of the garden to the continent. Building upon this foundation, students explore philosophy alongside patterns and methods of historical and contemporary practice. They develop their critical and research skills across the programme, in coordination with their studio work.

In the first year of the MLA, students undertake a comprehensive survey of landscape history that is both chronological and thematic. In the first year of the MA – the second year of the MLA – students develop essays from research seminars conducted in small groups led by specialist scholars. This year, topics have included extractivism and colonialism, creative and critical topographic practices, and ruins and ruination.

This study of history and theory culminates in the creation of the landscape thesis, completed with the guidance of dedicated supervisors. In this, students research a specific individual area of interest that informs and supports their design research.

In professional landscape architectural practice, much emphasis is placed upon communicating sophisticated understandings and complex strategies through documents which thoughtfully combine text and image. The thesis supports such integrative and synthetic work, and is itself a work of design, engaging students in the creation of a thesis book. The thesis supports the development of individual ideas and philosophies within the larger framework of landscape architecture history; current practice, politics and dwelling; and speculative features, near and far.

This year, the range of thesis topics was rich and fascinating, and many focused upon the topics addressed in a diverse set of research studios. Three theses are included for consideration here, their subjects all closely linked to the work of their respective studios. A representative excerpt of each has been provided. All these theses, as with so many others submitted, are rich both visually and textually, and designed with élan.

Seminar Leaders
Karen Fitzsimon, Eric Guibert, Danielle Hewitt, Will Jennings, Tiffany Kaewen Dang, Tom Keeley, Zoë Quick, Diana Salazar

Thesis Supervisors
Olivier Bellflamme, Albert Brenchat-Aguilar, Emma Colthurst, Gillian Darley, Paul Dobraszczyk, Kirti Durelle, Jon Goodbun, Eric Guibert, Danielle Hewitt, Will Jennings, Marko Jobst, Tom Keeley, Elin Eyborg Lund, Patrick Lynch, Hamish Muir, Andrew Ó Murchú, Anthony Powis, Zoë Quick, Jonathan Tyrell, Adam Walls, Stamatis Zografos

Flourishing through the Ashes: Mount Ymittos as a Landscape Ruin
Alexandra Souvatzi
Thesis Supervisor: Tom Keeley

This thesis employs a 'topographic practice' to perform a spatial investigation of Mount Ymittos – a mountain on the outskirts of contemporary Athens – which burns and is reborn through a cycle of fire. It does this in order to critically examine the mountain's role as a living ruin that relates to the city's historical and mythological past.

Walking was used as a medium to reveal a mnemonic system of places capable of linking the landscape with the Pyrocene and the Anthropocene. The selected route was dictated by firebreak roads created and maintained by the firefighting service, which run along the Mount and meet atmospheric units of different succession stages that are linked with the mythology, history, religion and politics of Athens.

As the walk was undertaken, Ymittos revealed some of its secrets and helped me comprehend its nature. On this route, myths and histories showed how the landscape was connected to past civilisations, a past whose importance is undermined. Through this I understood that Ymittos is a ruin of the Anthropocene, with traces of a long-lasting human activity visible in the landscape: in the extracted stones, the assigned paths and the constructed interventions. At the same time, Ymittos is constantly in a process of ruination, where cycles of fire and human engagement reshape its appearance and habitat. This Mount is not static; rather, it is a living landscape ruin.

The research began by investigating ways to stop the flames, but I now understand that this is not the solution. We're not separate from the world, or from the processes that nature has shaped to assist the chain of life. Perhaps, in our urge to find a new paradigm for the future, we should turn to our roots, to a time when Ymittos was indeed an extension of the city. The Mount might even have assisted Heraclitus when developing his philosophy, which suggested that fire is the end, but it is also the beginning.

Image: Psychogeography is combined with contemporary theories on fire management, attempting to reveal flaws of modernity, as well as to speculate upon a pyro-symbiotic future. Images by the author

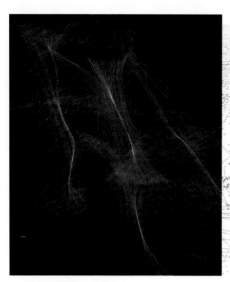
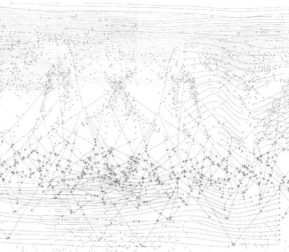

The Agency of Tópos
Dafni Filippa
Thesis Supervisor: Eric Guibert

This is not another study of emerging representation techniques in architectural and landscape disciplines. It is certainly not a quest to unveil state-of-the-art and visually attractive mediums (both digital and analogue) that inform the artistic aspirations of designers around the world, but rather a *work-in-progress* endeavour to test the ability of these mediums to match up with the synergetic complexity of their represented subjects.

As landscape architects, our main challenge is to build productive conditions that promote the biodiverse interaction of the central bodies that constitute the earthly biome: the ground (geosphere, hydrosphere), the atmosphere and the inhabitant species (biosphere). The way these systems bear upon or surface under the landscape and the boundless possibilities of their diachronic communication sets them into an ever-changing movement, a distinct 'agency' of their matter within a territorial context.

Every drawing we make to depict a design idea relies upon the successful representation of these spatial relationships, which are often generalised, abstracted to their core principles or visualised as stills in time, according to the relevant output we aim to communicate. This forms a significant conflict between theoretical ideas situated intellectually in the field of landscape architecture and their physical translation into drawing practices. Thus, isn't the medium of representation often limiting our ability to conceive a holistic perception of the dynamic entities concerned? How does this influence landscape practice as we transcend into an environmental and socio-political era of crisis, where landscape design, management and knowledge may become more crucial than ever before?

This essay's sections are arranged in an anti-stratigraphic way, with past representations and mediums rising to the surface first, while newer notions inscribe themselves more deeply. From this, the essay will propose a hybridised method of representing agency in topological organisations, not with the aim of depicting hyper-realistic conditions, but to provoke designers to use critical thinking and deploy drawing as an eidetic method in landscape practice.[1]

1. James Corner (1999), 'Eidetic Operations and New Landscapes'. In: A. B. Hirsch, ed. *Landscape Imagination: Collected Essays of James Corner 1990–2010.* New York: Princeton Architectural Press
Image: (L) Hybrid workflow using LIDAR point clouds and analogue drawing techniques to reveal agential representation practices. (R) The Epigenetic Landscape of W. H. Waddington, redrawn, to study the intra-action between Medium, Substance and Surfaces within topological organisations. Images by the author

Parys Mountain and the Human Body: A Photographic Analysis
Ziqi Niu
Thesis Supervisor: Zoë Quick

This essay tells the story of a modern wasteland, Parys Mountain in Wales, through a set of historical events. According to Vittoria Di Palma, 'wasteland' as a term was originally used to denote landscapes that 'stood apart from or outside the human culture'; however, it has since changed to mean 'sites that have been ravaged by industry'.[1] The shift in human attitude towards our place in nature speaks to the dramatic changes that have occurred in the past three centuries. Di Palma also states that 'to label landscapes as wastelands and to see it as a problem with a solution is not a concept found across different times and places'.[2]

Furthermore, Raymond Williams' critique on culture declares that 'the idea of nature contains, though often unnoticed, an extraordinary amount of human history'.[3] The act of tapping into the history of a specific site of 'nature' is a cultural act that redefines the way we perceive and understand our surroundings. Through this act, we can evaluate the human assumptions and beliefs that unavoidably influence the shape of nature.

Photography has been a driving force that has been able to capture and define various forms of aesthetics of landscapes. This thesis addresses Parys Mountain through different lenses: first as a landscape of production, then as a landscape of the sublime and finally as a landscape of change. Each form of the landscape is analysed using photography, giving an insight into what the landscape meant for humans at that time. The thesis unpacks the changing ways in which humans have related to the landscape of extraction through the evolution of photographs in Parys Mountain. Through this structure, the essay identifies future perspectives and opportunities in addressing post-extractive landscapes with creative practices such as landscape architecture.

1. Vittoria Di Palma (2014), *Wasteland: A History*, New Haven: Yale University Press
2. Di Palma (2014), *Wasteland: A History*
3. Raymond Williams (2005), *Culture and Materialism: Selected Essays*, London: Verso
Image: View of Parys Mountain, 2022. Image by the author

Design studies in progress in the Landscape Architecture
studio. Photo: Zifeng Ye

ucl.ac.uk/architecture
bartlettarchucl.com
Find us on 🅕 🅨 🅞 🆅 ▶

Publisher
The Bartlett School of Architecture, UCL

Editor
Srijana Gurung

Proofreader
Karen Francis

Graphic Design
Patrick Morrissey, Unlimited
weareunlimited.co.uk

Executive Editors
Penelope Haralambidou,
Amy Kulper

Bartlett life photography included taken
by Bartlett tutors and students.

ISBN 978-1-8383185-9-8

The Bartlett School of Architecture, UCL
22 Gordon Street
London WC1H 0QB

+44 (0)20 3108 9646
architecture@ucl.ac.uk